MAY 2 1 2018

SUPER SIMPLE
EARTH INVESTIGATIONS

SUPER SIMPLE
VOLCANO
PROJECTS

Science Activities for
Future Volcanologists

JESSIE ALKIRE

CONSULTING EDITOR, DIANE CRAIG, M.A./READING SPECIALIST

Super Sandcastle

An Imprint of Abdo Publishing
abdopublishing.com

abdopublishing.com

Published by Abdo Publishing, a division of ABDO, PO Box 398166, Minneapolis, Minnesota 55439. Copyright © 2018 by Abdo Consulting Group, Inc. International copyrights reserved in all countries. No part of this book may be reproduced in any form without written permission from the publisher. Super SandCastle™ is a trademark and logo of Abdo Publishing.

Printed in the United States of America, North Mankato, Minnesota
102017
012018

THIS BOOK CONTAINS RECYCLED MATERIALS

Design: Kelly Doudna, Mighty Media, Inc.
Production: Mighty Media, Inc.
Editor: Liz Salzmann
Cover Photographs: Mighty Media, Inc.; Shutterstock
Interior Photographs: Courtesy of the U.S. Geological Survey; iStockphoto; Mighty Media, Inc.; Science Source; Shutterstock

The following manufacturers/names appearing in this book are trademarks: Aleene's® Original Tacky Glue®, Arm & Hammer™, Coca-Cola®, Colgate®, Dawn®, Elmer's® Glue-All®, Gedney®, Pyrex®, Quaker®, Reynolds® Cut-Rite®, Westcott® KleenCut®

Publisher's Cataloging-in-Publication Data
Names: Alkire, Jessie, author.
Title: Super simple volcano projects: science activities for future volcanologists / by Jessie Alkire.
Other titles: Science activities for future volcanologists
Description: Minneapolis, Minnesota : Abdo Publishing, 2018. | Series: Super simple earth investigations
Identifiers: LCCN 2017946520 | ISBN 9781532112409 (lib.bdg.) | ISBN 9781614799825 (ebook)
Subjects: LCSH: Volcanological research--Juvenile literature. | Earth sciences--Juvenile literature. | Science--Experiments--Juvenile literature.
Classification: DDC 507.8--dc23
LC record available at https://lccn.loc.gov/2017946520

Super SandCastle™ books are created by a team of professional educators, reading specialists, and content developers around five essential components—phonemic awareness, phonics, vocabulary, text comprehension, and fluency—to assist young readers as they develop reading skills and strategies and increase their general knowledge. All books are written, reviewed, and leveled for guided reading and early reading intervention programs for use in shared, guided, and independent reading and writing activities to support a balanced approach to literacy instruction.

TO ADULT HELPERS

The projects in this title are fun and simple. There are just a few things to remember to keep kids safe. Some projects require the use of sharp objects. Also, kids may be using messy materials such as glue or paint. Make sure they protect their clothes and work surfaces. Review the projects before starting, and be ready to assist when necessary.

KEY SYMBOL

Watch for this warning symbol in this book. Here is what it means.

SHARP!
You will be working with a sharp object. Get help!

CONTENTS

WHAT IS A VOLCANO?

A volcano is a vent or opening in Earth's surface. Melted rock rises through a **conduit** from Earth's **interior** to the surface. This melted rock is called magma. Magma is very hot. It can be hotter than 2,000 **degrees** Fahrenheit (1,100°C)!

A volcano can erupt. This is when magma comes out of the volcano. After it comes out of a volcano, magma is called lava. Gas and rock can also come out of a volcano during an eruption. Eruptions can cause **damage** and hurt people.

MAGMA

MOUNT ETNA, ITALY

After an eruption, the lava hardens into a layer of rock around the vent. Each time a volcano erupts, a new layer is added.

The top of a volcano has a crater. This is a low, bowl-shaped area. The vent is in the bottom of the crater.

Some volcanoes are tens of thousands of years old. They have erupted many times. The layers of hardened lava have made them into tall mountains!

KARYMSKY VOLCANO, RUSSIA

TYPES OF VOLCANOES

There are three main types of volcanoes. They are shield volcanoes, composite volcanoes, and **cinder** cones.

SHIELD VOLCANO

Shield volcanoes are very wide with gradual slopes. These volcanoes have thin, runny lava. Thin lava travels farther than thick lava. This lava hardens and forms the volcano's wide shape. Mauna Loa in Hawaii is a shield volcano.

COMPOSITE VOLCANO

Most composite volcanoes are very tall mountains. These volcanoes are covered with layers of hardened lava, ash, and rocks. Their eruptions are the most powerful. Mount Fuji in Japan is a composite volcano.

CINDER CONE

Cinder cones are small cone-shaped volcanoes. They are made of loose cinder. Some cinder cones form on the sides of larger volcanoes. Sunset Crater in Arizona is a cinder cone.

HOW SCIENTISTS STUDY VOLCANOES

S ome scientists study volcanoes. They are called volcanologists.

Volcanologists look at how volcanoes work. They learn why volcanoes erupt. They try to **predict** eruptions. This gives people time to move to safe areas.

Volcanologists record eruptions. They study rock and lava samples. They measure ground movement, temperature, and more.

Volcanologists also watch a volcano's shape. Changes can mean an eruption is coming!

A VOLCANOLOGIST COLLECTS SAMPLES OF HOT LAVA.

MAURICE & KATIA KRAFFT

Maurice and Katia Krafft were volcanologists. They met in college and later married in 1970. The Kraffts traveled the world studying volcanoes. They filmed many eruptions. In 1991, the couple filmed Mount Unzen's eruption in Japan. They were killed in the eruption.

MOUNT UNZEN, JAPAN

ASIA

JAPAN

MOUNT UNZEN

MATERIALS

Here are some of the materials that you will need for the projects in this book.

BAKING SODA

COLORED PAPER

CRAFT FOAM

CRAFT GLUE

DENTAL FLOSS

DISH SOAP

FELT

FOOD COLORING

GRAHAM CRACKERS

LIQUID MEASURING CUP

MASKING TAPE

MEASURING SPOONS

TIPS AND TECHNIQUES

MODELING CLAY	**MOSS**	**NAIL**	**PLASTIC PLATE**
PLASTIC WRAP	**PLIERS**	**ROUND CARDBOARD CONTAINER**	**SHALLOW CARDBOARD BOX**
SMOOTH-SIDED JAR	**TOOTHPASTE**	**VINEGAR**	**WAX PAPER**

Modeling clay is great for volcano projects. But modeling clay is tough and stiff. You need to work the clay with your hands to soften it. Squeeze and stretch it until it's easy to shape. Once softened, modeling clay can be shaped into a volcano or any clay creation!

COLORFUL EARTH LAYERS

MATERIALS: modeling clay (yellow, orange, red, brown, blue & green), wax paper, smooth-sided jar, dental floss

Earth is made of four main layers. These are the inner **core**, outer core, mantle, and crust. Magma is melted rock from the mantle. The crust includes layers of rock and dirt that make up the continents. The oceans sit on top of the crust. They fill the spaces between the continents.

EARTH LAYER KEY

YELLOW = INNER CORE	RED = MANTLE
ORANGE = OUTER CORE	BROWN & GREEN = CRUST
	BLUE = OCEAN

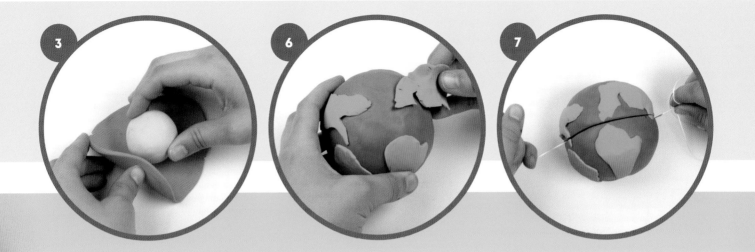

① Roll six balls of clay. Make them different sizes. The green and yellow balls should be the smallest. The orange and red should be medium-sized. And the brown and blue should be the largest.

② Set the orange ball on a sheet of wax paper. Use the jar to flatten the ball.

③ Wrap the orange clay around the yellow ball. Roll the ball to smooth it.

④ Flatten the red ball. Wrap it over the orange clay. Add the brown and blue clay the same way.

⑤ Break the green ball into smaller pieces. Flatten the pieces and form them into the shapes of continents.

⑥ Press the green shapes onto the ball. These represent areas where the crust rises above the ocean to form continents.

⑦ Use dental floss to cut the clay ball in half. Pull the halves apart. You can see the layers of Earth!

FELT VOLCANO

MATERIALS: scissors, ruler, light brown felt, craft glue, large sheet of craft foam, dark brown felt, marker, masking tape, red felt, light gray felt, plain paper

A volcano changes each time it erupts. But each eruption has the same basic features.

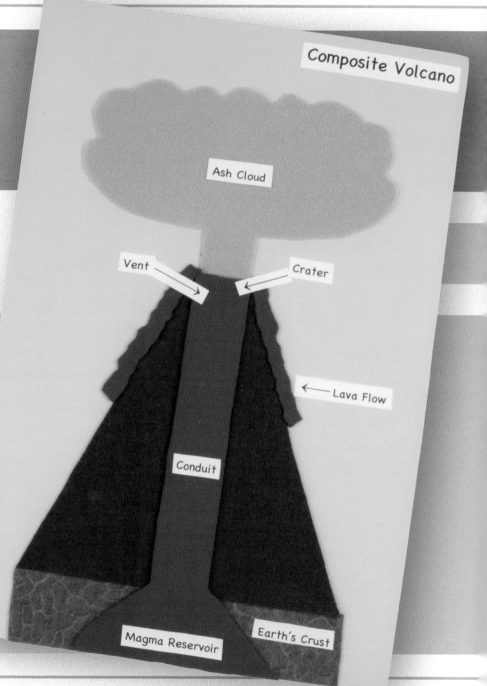

Composite Volcano

Ash Cloud

Vent

Crater

Lava Flow

Conduit

Magma Reservoir

Earth's Crust

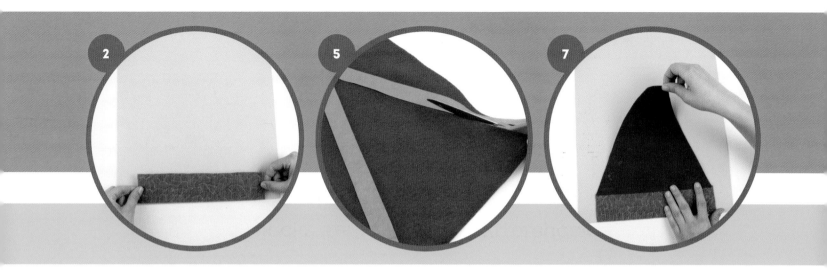

1. Cut a rectangle out of light brown felt. Make it 9 by 2 inches (23 by 5 cm). This is Earth's crust.

2. Glue Earth's crust along the bottom edge of the craft foam.

3. Find the center of a short side of the dark brown felt. Draw a dot 1½ inches (4 cm) in from the edge.

4. Use masking tape to make a line from the dot to each opposite corner.

5. Cut along the inside of the tape. This triangle is the volcano.

6. Cut off the top corner of the volcano.

7. Glue the volcano above Earth's crust.

8. Measure the distance from the bottom of the crust to the top of the volcano.

9. Cut a piece of red felt and two pieces of masking tape as long as the measurement.

Continued on the next page.

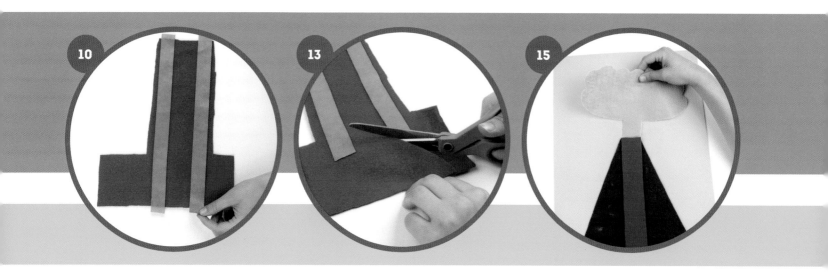

10 Stick the pieces of masking tape side by side on the red felt. Place them 1½ inches (4 cm) apart.

11 Make a mark at the bottom of the felt 1½ inches (4 cm) to the left of the left piece of tape. Make a mark at the bottom of the felt 1½ inches (4 cm) to the right of the right piece of tape.

12 Cut 2 inches (5 cm) off the bottom of each piece of tape.

13 Cut from the right mark to the inside of the right piece of tape. Cut along the inside of the tape to the top of the felt. Cut the left side the same way.

14 Glue the red felt shape on top of the volcano. The narrow column is the volcano's **conduit**. The triangle at the bottom is the magma **reservoir**.

15 Cut a cloud shape out of light gray felt. This is the ash cloud. Glue it above the volcano.

16 Make paper labels for each part of the volcano. Glue them to the volcano.

DIGGING DEEPER

The main parts of a volcano are the magma **reservoir**, **conduit**, and vent. Magma from the magma reservoir rises through the conduit. It is released through the vent at the top of the conduit. A cloud of ash and gases is also released. This is an eruption!

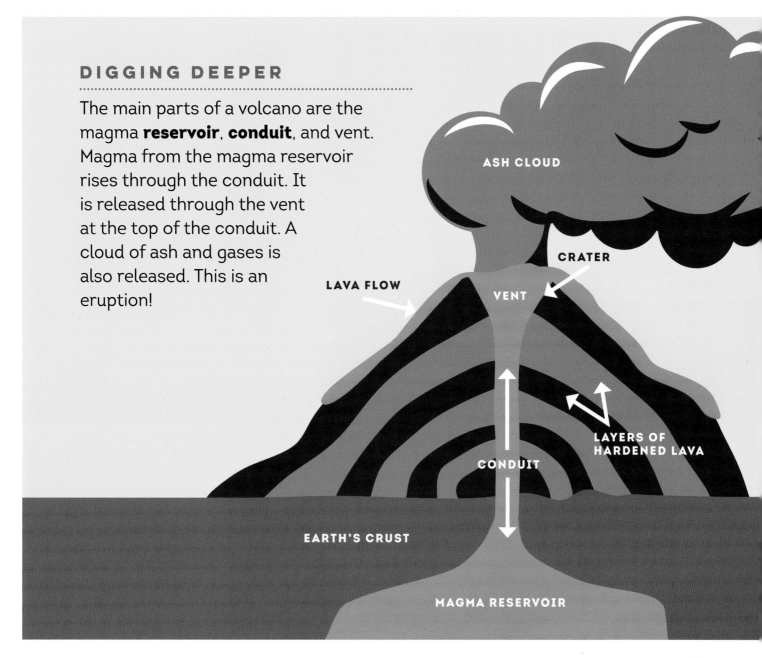

ASH CLOUD

CRATER

LAVA FLOW

VENT

LAYERS OF HARDENED LAVA

CONDUIT

EARTH'S CRUST

MAGMA RESERVOIR

TOOTHPASTE MAGMA

MATERIALS: round cardboard container, ruler, scissors, colored paper, clear tape, plastic wrap, nail, graham crackers, modeling clay, toothpaste

Earth's crust is made of rock. Magma pushes through the crust toward Earth's surface. This can make the ground rise!

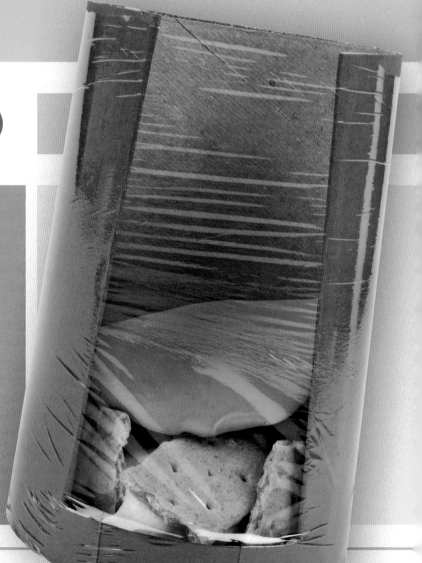

1 Make two cuts from the top of the container almost to the bottom. Space them 3 inches (8 cm) apart.

2 Cut across from the end of one cut to the end of the other cut. Remove the piece you cut out. Cover the container with colored paper.

3 Tape plastic wrap over the opening.

4 Use a nail to poke a hole in the bottom of the container. Make the hole as big as the toothpaste tube's opening.

5 Put several layers of graham crackers in the container. These are the layers of rock in Earth's crust.

6 Flatten the clay into a circle as big as the top of the container. Place it on top of the graham crackers. This is Earth's surface.

7 Take the cap off the toothpaste. Push the opening into the hole in the container.

8 Squeeze the toothpaste tube hard. The toothpaste magma pushes through the cracker layers to the surface!

BUBBLY ERUPTING VOLCANO

MATERIALS: pliers, empty soda can, modeling clay, wax paper, smooth-sided jar, newspaper, plastic plate, hot tap water, liquid measuring cup, measuring spoons, dish soap, red food coloring, baking soda, spoon, vinegar

Sometimes volcanoes erupt. Lava comes out of the volcano's crater. Rocks, gas, and ash do too. These **substances** can harm nature, people, and structures.

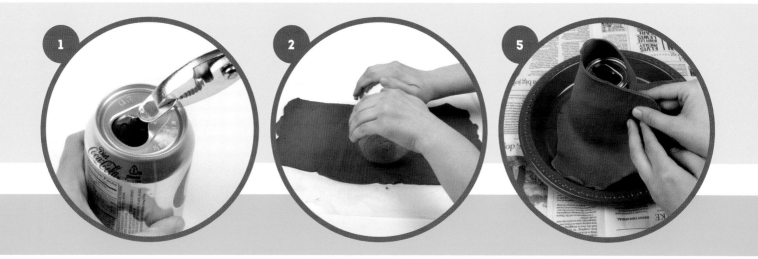

1 Use a pliers to remove the tab from the soda can. Pull on the edges of the hole to make it bigger.

2 Work the clay to soften it. Place the clay on a sheet of wax paper. Use the jar to roll the clay flat.

③ Cover your work surface with newspaper.

④ Set the plate on the newspaper. Set the can on the plate. The can will be the inside of the volcano.

5 Mold the clay around the soda can so it forms a cone shape. Leave an opening at the top.

⑥ Pinch the clay to give it a bumpy surface like a real volcano.

Continued on the next page.

⑦ Fill a liquid measuring cup with 1 cup of hot tap water.

⑧ Add a tablespoon of dish soap.

⑨ Add several drops of red food coloring. The mixture should be dark red.

⑩ Add 2 tablespoons of baking soda.

⑪ Stir gently until the baking soda **dissolves**.

⑫ Pour the mixture into the soda can.

⑬ Add vinegar to the soda can until your volcano erupts!

DIGGING DEEPER

A volcano's shape is made by eruptions. A volcano starts as an opening in the ground. The **substances** released in an eruption cool and harden. This creates the volcano's shape. The volcano gets bigger with each eruption!

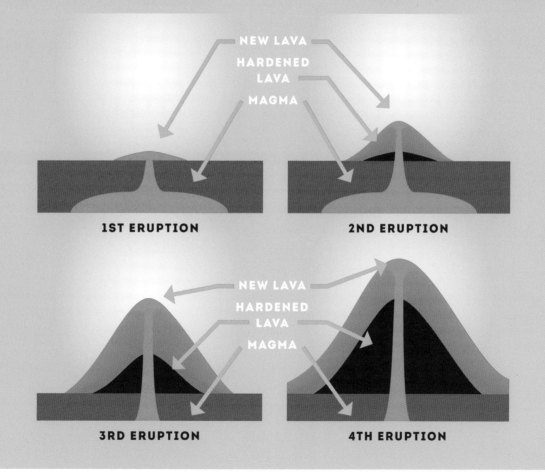

CLAY SHIELD VOLCANO

MATERIALS: craft glue, green paper, cardboard, scissors, modeling clay (green & red), wax paper, smooth-sided jar, pencil

Shield volcanoes can be miles wide! They erupt more often than other volcanoes. But the eruptions are usually mild.

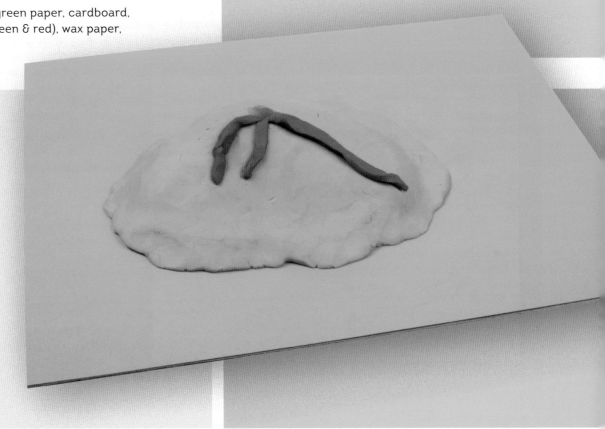

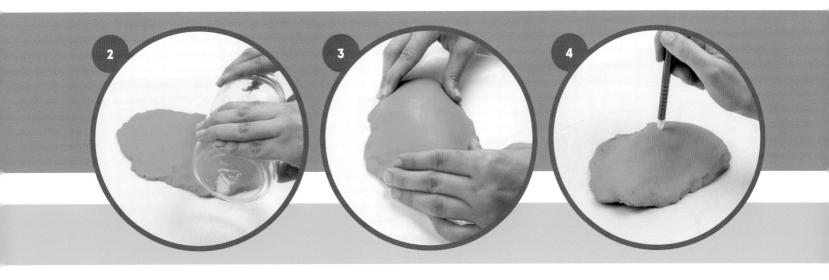

① Glue green paper to a large piece of cardboard. Trim the edges if needed.

② Work the green clay to soften it. Place the clay on a sheet of wax paper. Use the jar to roll the clay flat.

③ Mold the clay into a low hill shape. This is a shield volcano.

④ Make a hole in the top of the volcano with a pencil.

⑤ Place the volcano on the piece of cardboard. Press the volcano's edges down firmly.

⑥ Work the red clay to soften it. Break the clay into pieces. Flatten the pieces of red clay into long strips.

⑦ Put one end of each strip in the hole. Press the strips into the sides of the volcano. These are lava flows.

VOLCANO LANDSCAPE DIORAMA

MATERIALS: shallow cardboard box with an open top, ruler, green & blue paper, scissors, craft glue, modeling clay (black & red), wax paper, smooth-sided jar, marker, soil, moss, plain paper

A volcano changes the area surrounding it. Its eruptions can form lakes, islands, rocks, and soil.

Lava Flow

Volcano

Volcanic Lake

Volcanic Ash & Soil

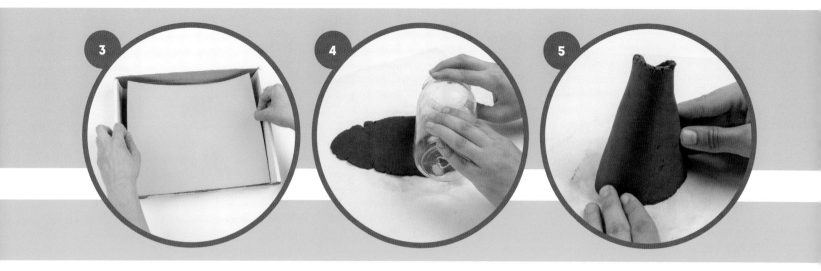

① Measure the bottom of your box.

② Cut a piece of green paper to fit the measurements.

③ Glue the paper to the bottom of the box. This is the ground.

④ Work the black clay to soften it. Place the clay on a sheet of wax paper. Use the jar to roll the clay flat.

⑤ Mold the black clay into a cone-shaped volcano. Leave an opening at the top for the crater.

⑥ Place the volcano in a corner of the box. Press the bottom of the volcano down firmly so it stays in place.

Continued on the next page.

(7) Work the red clay to soften it. Break the clay into pieces. Flatten the pieces of red clay into long strips.

(8) Put one end of each strip in the top of the volcano. Press the strips into the sides. These are lava flows.

(9) Draw a lake on blue paper. Cut it out.

(10) Glue the lake onto the ground near the volcano. This is a volcanic lake.

(11) Sprinkle soil around the volcano and the ground. This is volcanic soil and ash.

(12) Place moss on the ground and in the soil.

(13) Make paper labels for each part of the volcano scene. Glue them in place.

DIGGING DEEPER

Two types of volcanic lakes are crater lakes and maars. A crater lake forms when rocks fall from the sides of the crater to the bottom. The rocks block the vent. This creates a bowl that can hold water and form a lake.

A maar forms when magma near Earth's surface touches underground water. This causes an explosion of steam. The explosion creates a crater on the ground. The crater can fill with water, creating a maar.

MAAR FORMATION

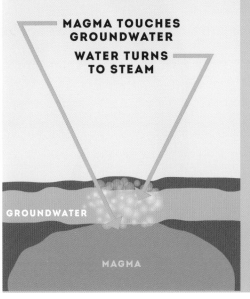

MAGMA TOUCHES
GROUNDWATER
WATER TURNS
TO STEAM

GROUNDWATER

MAGMA

STEAM EXPLODES
CRATER FORMS

GROUNDWATER

MAGMA

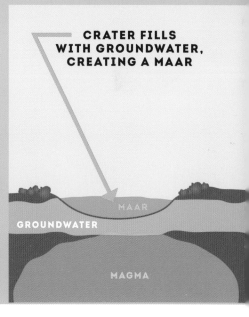

CRATER FILLS
WITH GROUNDWATER,
CREATING A MAAR

GROUNDWATER

MAAR

MAGMA

CONCLUSION

It is important to understand volcanoes. They are found all over the world! Volcanoes can cause a lot of **damage**. Volcanologists study volcanoes. They **predict** eruptions and save lives.

QUIZ

1. What is melted rock in Earth's **interior** called?

2. **Cinder** cones are the largest volcanoes.
   TRUE OR FALSE?

3. Which volcano were the Kraffts filming when they died?

LEARN MORE ABOUT IT!

You can find out more about volcanoes at the library. Or you can ask an adult to help you **research** volcanoes **online**!

Answers: 1. Magma   2. False   3. Mount Unzen

GLOSSARY

cinder – a small piece of ash or cooled lava.

conduit – a pipe or tube through which something passes.

core – the center of a space object such as a planet, moon, or star.

damage – harm or ruin.

degree – the unit used to measure temperature.

dissolve – to become part of a liquid.

interior – the area inside something.

online – connected to the Internet.

predict – to say what will happen in the future.

research – to find out more about something.

reservoir – a place where a liquid is stored.

substance – anything that takes up space, such as a solid object or a liquid.